THE ANIMAL BOOK

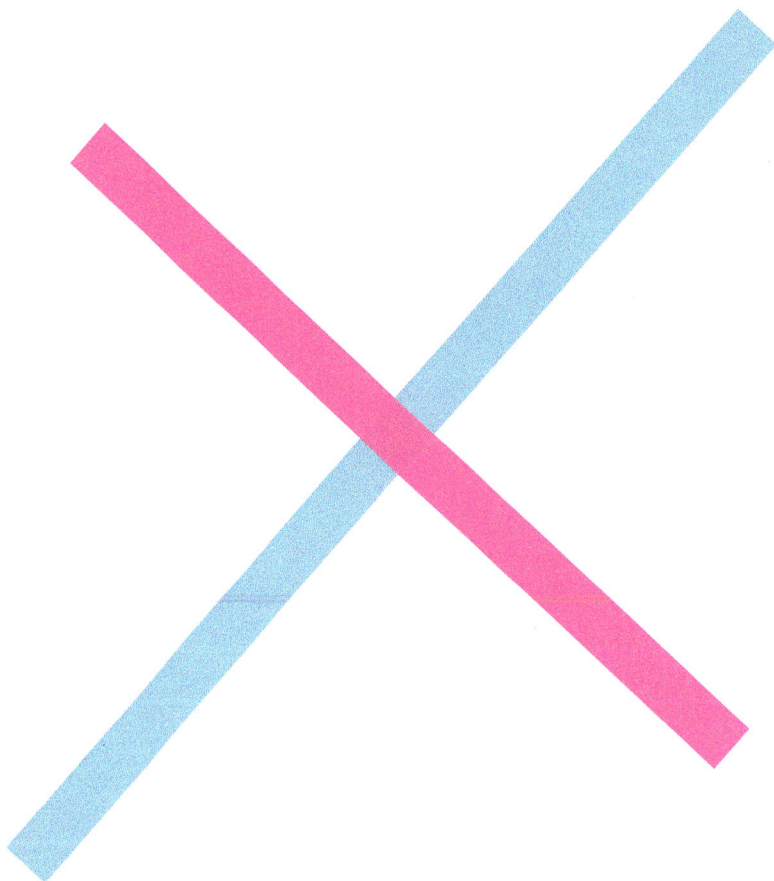

MICHAEL HARREN
THE ANIMAL BOOK

introduction by
Adam Fitzgerald

bd
nyc

The Animal Book

The Animal Book is based on *The Animal Show*, which has been performed in venues throughout the United States. An album of music from the show is also available.

Published by bd-studios.com in New York City, 2018

Introduction © Adam Fitzgerald

All photography © Michael Harren except as noted below:
Diane Bezanski — Cover, 8, 132
Anonymous — 100-107
Donna Harren — 31
Gabrielle Stubbert — 22-23, 41-5
Unparalleled Suffering Photography — 62-5
Seth Webster — 34-6, 39, 50-9, 86-7, 94-5, 109-20

Art Direction and Design by luke kurtis

ISBN 978-0-9992078-4-0

For Tilly

CONTENTS

In the Fall of 2014, I took a road trip to Woodstock Farm Animal Sanctuary with my friends Ethan Ciment and Michael Suchman. If you don't already know about these two, collectively known as The Vegan Mos, I suggest you correct that at once. This was my first trip to Woodstock's annual "Thanksliving" celebration, and it was my first chance to take a breather after the release of my first book and album project, *Tentative Armor*.

Speaking of firsts, *Tentative Armor* was my first solo show, too, and I have to admit that the whole thing felt like a fluke—an accident. I knew I had done it, and I knew that experience had been real, but it was hard to believe that I had made that thing, and especially hard to believe that I might be able to make another thing. Before *Tentative Armor*, I had only ever performed other people's work from my usual spot, tucked away at the piano. *Tentative Armor* had been my first attempt to move center stage with my own writing. How could someone like me manage something like that again?

The trip to Woodstock was as glorious as I expected: lots of rescued animals, lots of compassionate vegan folks, and of course, lots of food. The turkeys are the guests of honor at this Thanksgiving celebration, so before the humans commence their plant-based feast, everyone gathers around while the Turkeys enjoy their own feast. It was a beautiful reminder of why places like this exist: to protect these precious animals from us. Even though I had already been an ethical vegan for a few years at that point, I had very limited experience with the animals whom I used to regard as food, especially in their alive and sentient state. I found it tremendously moving that this place existed solely to provide a home and care for these animals who were rescued from being killed and eaten.

After our feast, the founders of the sanctuary, Jenny Brown and Doug Abel, made an announcement: the sanctuary was moving to a new, massive location. This meant, of course, more space for the animals and those who cared for them, but also, more space for visitors and long term guests. There would be dorms for long term volunteers, a retreat program for animal allies, educational outreach for visiting school groups, and beyond! While the other attendees cheered for this exciting development for the sanctuary, I had the spark of what became The Animal Show: could I be a resident artist at an animal sanctuary?

I went to work on designing a proposal with another good friend, David Cabrera. I planned to spend a year volunteering as much as possible at a sanctuary, working with the animals, collecting video, audio and stories. I would create my own experience about which to write the new show. Around the time I realized my proposal wouldn't be a good fit for Woodstock, I heard about a newer sanctuary in northern New Jersey.

At first glance, Tamerlaine Farm was a simple chicken sanctuary which, in all honesty, seemed boring. What in the world could I possibly write about chickens? Even as an already passionate vegan, I didn't care much about chickens. Weren't they just little egg laying robots?

More and more though, the universe seemed to point me toward Tamerlaine Farm. I ran into co-founder Peter Nussbaum at some Veg Fest or other, already acquainted with him through my running team, Strong Hearts Vegan Power. Soon after that, I met his wife, Gabrielle, at another Veg Fest (we vegans and our Veg Fests, am I right?). I hesitantly mentioned my artist residency idea to her, and she was remarkably enthusiastic. Peter and I wound up sharing a hotel room during a race, and we discussed it a little more. Though I still didn't know what it would be, this thing was beginning.

In September of 2015, my Artist Residency began at Tamerlaine Farm Animal Sanctuary. As you'll discover in this book, this experience was the catalyst for a deeper awareness about non-human animals, and a strengthening of my resolve to fight for them. Peter and Gabrielle have become two of my closest friends. I love them dearly, and I love the place they created at Tamerlaine Farm.

I hope your will enjoy your experience with the words and photographs contained in these pages, and with the music and words on the accompanying album. I hope it makes you think about how you view our fellow earthlings, and inspires you to consider them more carefully with the decisions you make each day. We truly are all one.

For the animals,
Michael Harren

Collaboration with Michael Harren has been, and continues to be, among the great pleasures of my work as an artist over the past decade. I have been fortunate to work with Michael on multiple projects and on a wide range of theatrical, musical, and multimedia endeavors over the years. We have been exchanging and co-creating for such a long time and in so many ways that I would be hard pressed to make a complete list of everything we have made together, and I look forward to many more. That said...

The Animal Show is different.

The Animal Show is more important.

The Animal Show is an example of what every artist hopes to do: effectively and beautifully combine art and activism to deliver an honest, creative, moving, and informative piece of work aimed at changing minds.

It is no easy feat to change what and how people eat. Food is woven intricately into the fabric of an individual's history, culture, sense of comfort, routine, family, and fundamental happiness. To tell a person they should and must give up the consumption of animals is to tell that person that their daily activities, their holidays, their enjoyment, and their sustenance are violent, destructive, and morally bankrupt. It is not an easy message to deliver, and the resistance to hearing that message is strong.

I work with Michael on his projects of artivism because he has, as so few do, an incredible ability to create work that both touches its audience on an emotional level and appeals to those same people on an intellectual one. The stereotype of the "angry vegan" exists partially because those fighting against the mass slaughter of animals are, rightfully, angry and partially because carnivorous humans do not want to hear about their own destructive behavior. Michael has an amazing ability to traverse both worlds and hold on to his passion and anger while delivering a message of love and compassion through music, storytelling, and performance.

I was a meat eater when I met Michael. I am now a vegetarian veering toward a life free of animal-product consumption. I cannot say it is all Michael's doing, but I know that his patient, passionate, never-ending commitment to animals and the stunning art he creates driven by those principles have changed my mind, my habits, and my life. I am honored to have worked with Michael on this show. I am a better artist and, hopefully, a better human as a result.

I hope you enjoy the work Michael has created. I hope you take it in, process it, read the words, hear the music, and revel in the beauty. I hope it makes you think. I hope it makes you change. I know it did for me.

Adam Fitzgerald
Director, Collaborator, and Friend

CASEY

You are
Aloft in straw
And safe
Feathers, folded frayed and
Broken
Breed betrayed
But blessed by
Hands like mine that
Know and see and wonder.

I did not know you 'till
Today I do and did and
Will forever feel
Your face in my hand
Your trust in my kind—
The few of us who see
You are you like
I am me

I do not know where you were
Before
Nor you my history seen
But here are two souls
Touching
Eye to eye
Face to hand
Soul to soul

You are broken
As am I
In this moment:
Whole.

TREES BREATHE HARMONY

I'm here.

It's my first visit to Tamerlaine Farm. I'm here and it's summer and I'm hot, which I hate.

But... I'm here. Gabrielle and Peter started this place a few years ago with two roosters, Yuri and Jupiter. It must have been right, because the place has grown to be a home for pigs, goats, ducks, turkeys, a huge flock of chickens, oh, and two dogs, Tonka and Lola.

I've been thinking about animals a lot lately.

Why they do what they do and why we do what we do to them. I knew this was a place where they were cared for and kept safe from us. We like to use them but not here.

There's the yard of roosters called the frat house. I don't know them that well yet, so I walk in without fear. I'm still wearing my rose-colored "these animals know what an awesome vegan human I am" glasses but they're here and they are allowed to be who they are which means... In a couple of days they might decide they're tired of me. That's the way it goes. This is *their* yard. Not mine.

Here, there's another yard of chickens, maybe 70 of them. Rescued from being gassed when they were no longer useful as laying hens. They were objects there, in those battery cages... but here? They have names. *Names.* Every single one of them. I am awestruck when I see Maggie, the caregiver, enter the yard and reflexively tell me the names of these chickens. One after the other. She knows them all. There are others here who survived ritual sacrifice. Miraculously they were not slaughtered in the streets of Brooklyn. Their throats were not slit, their still conscious bodies were not tossed into a garbage bag and left to bleed out while they wondered:

That was life?

No. They're *here*, and this is life.This place exists for them and their safety and their person and their names...

Turkey   Lemon   Jonathan   Gertrude

Rose   Jeremiah   Curi   Ricky   Eli   JW

Atlantis   Rebel   Piper   Tara   Tessa

Brutus   Sid   Maizy   Lennon   Vince

Dottie   Mia   Kit   Vivianne   Tilda

Benjamin   George   Anthony   Alvin

Simon   Theodore   Gus   Seymour

Larry   Gidget   Teddy   Keiko   Ms

Daisy   Fern   Penny Brown   Snow

Suzie   Mickey   Juliette   Chip

Mrs. Green   Fiona   Ned   Dusty

Arianna   Stitches   Jewel   Elise

Petra   Caroline   Mabel   Daria   Gil

Aerosmith   Kiska   Delilah   Luna

Mond   Mahina   Muezi   Ming

Ming   Grandpa   Grandma   Cole

Elliot Elle Neptune Phyllis Pierre

Daisy Crystal Bubbles Hector

Mindy Virginia Lois Bertha Squirt

Esther Felipe Betsy Dove Stoney

Joe Buddy Dom Simon Asia

Beatrice Belinda Brooklyn Carla

Donna Dorothy Duckie Eleanor

Flavia Francesca Furiosa Grace

Henry Holly Ida Irena Jacob

Julia Kiki Klara Koko Krishna

Lara Lettie Lion Lourdes Mandy

Maria Martina Naomi Olga

Paco Paula Petra Piper Polly

Polona Rosalie Scar Scarecrow

Serena Shakira Shelby Sila

Sylvia Toad Victoria Violet

CORKY

I was 10 years old, on the cusp of middle school with the taste of adolescence on my tongue. It was the year before my parents divorce and two years before my first piano. My best friends were The Muppets, who I watched on our rabbit-eared black and white TV that sat perched on the olive green kitchen counter. My big dream at the time was to be hospitalized for some ailment that was bad enough to land me in the hospital, but not so bad that I couldn't watch *The Muppet Show* on the color TVs I'd heard equipped each room. Those were the days when my friend Brenda and I used to make fake braces for our teeth out of paper clips, and we would sometimes throw ourselves out of the tall tree in her front yard, hoping to break a leg or at least sprain an ankle so we could go to school the next day on crutches, or better yet, in a wheelchair. I guess you could consider that a somewhat desperate plan just to get a little attention, but we thought being somehow... defective... would be really, really cool.

I carried my Muppets lunchbox back and forth to school each day with pride. I knew the show was for adults too, so I felt a little superior to my classmates who mocked me for carrying what was, to them, something for little kids. Most of the boys in my Houston suburb were really into BMX bikes, and the girls? Well, I was just too excited that they were willing to sit out in the furthest reaches of the playground with me singing Barry Manilow tunes to really worry about what lunch box designs they were into.

One day as I walked home from school, I ran across a little matted up dog who I almost immediately named "Corky." She was some kind of Yorkshire Terrier and Pekingese mix who took ownership of me the moment I stopped and pet her. She followed me all the way home and I gave her something to eat, maybe half of my Little Debbie Star Crunch, or something equally appropriate for a hungry stray dog. I waited until my mom came home to start my campaign to allow Corky to live with us, which was a surprisingly easy sell. The one requirement was that we put Corky back outside for a little while in case she wanted to go back to her *real* home.

So we did, and I probably nagged my mother every minute on the minute to go out and see if Corky was still there. When she finally relented, I darted outside calling into the thick Texas dusk:

"CORKY!" "CORKY!"

"CORKY!"

There was no sign of her. I walked around the block a bit, hoping to see her nose poking out beneath a hedge. Nothing.

Almost defeated, I headed back home and back up our driveway. My final call...

"Corky?" caught in my throat and just as I started to cry, I caught some movement in the corner of my eye under our diarrhea green VW van, and there she was, with a hopeful look that seemed to ask, "Are you talking to me?"

That's how our friendship began, Corky and me, and it was a good one. Even though we had a backyard, I happily took her on walks every day when I got home from school. That's a pretty big deal for a kid who was as *indoorsy* as me. I dutifully brushed her hair (when I remembered) and only got grossed out a little when pieces of her shit got matted up in the long hair on her hindquarters. My brother started calling those "Corkyberries," which sometimes makes me giggle to this day.

As I got older and my adolescent awkwardness grew, so did my love for and connection with Corky. When a not-even-from-this-neighborhood kid spit on me and punched me in the face as I walked home from school, Corky was waiting for me when I got there. When the alcoholism in my household came to a head, when my parents divorced, when my brother moved out... I had consistency in my friend. Corky didn't even seem to mind that I was starting to notice the fit of the other boy's underwear in the locker room after gym class, or my secret stash of crude original drawings of male nudes.

I had a particularly surprising moment in gym class that year. I'll spare you the cliche details of how I was picked last and begrudgingly accepted by my new touch football teammates who got stuck with me. I didn't then, nor do I really know now, the intricacies of football, touch or otherwise, so I wasn't exactly sure why I was chasing this kid other than the fact that he was holding the ball and I was pretty sure he was on the other team. The surprising thing was that I was keeping up with him, and close enough to tag him out.

"If you tag me, I'll kick your ass," he said.

So I didn't. I ran right behind him laughing a little nervously, but really more than anything I was thrilled that I was doing something sports-y and doing well enough that I could win something against this jock kid. I kept running, gleefully behind him as he crossed that touchdown line thingy and scored a number of points that remains a mystery. I was high on that moment for a good fifteen seconds until I saw the faces of my teammates. They were not happy like I was that I could just keep up with jock kid. They wanted me to tag him and keep him from scoring against us. It was obvious that I could have stopped him, "so why didn't you, faggot?"

I walked home from school that day alone, ashamed of being afraid to tag jock kid.

Somewhere inside that word "faggot" resonated, even though I didn't know yet that I was, indeed, a faggot. I knew that there was something about me that wasn't right, that was... off.

As I unlocked and opened the door, my parents were divorced by now and my mom was at work, the absence hit me. For all of the years I knew her, Corky greeted me when I came home, leaping and yapping at my legs and hoping for a walk. In this moment it especially stung to remember that she was gone. Our neighbor's dog jumped over the fence pretty frequently, and it was always pretty harmless until this one Saturday when they were fighting over a bone, and the dog from next door picked up Corky in his mouth and gave her a vicious shake. She died the next day.

In these after-school moments when I was the only one home, her absence was more pronounced than ever. Had she still been around, we would have gone for a walk and then sat in the big black chair in front of the tv. She would nestle in between my leg and the chair's arm and we would spend that sacred time home alone together. But not today. The sting of "faggot" and the pall of grief stood me in front of the bathroom mirror, sobbing into a towel in case someone came home. I was *really* alone.

HOME AGAIN

Yes it was a long time
Yes it was a dream
The kind you find inside your world
Nestled in between
The fear and hesitation
Suspicion and distrust
Growing out of boyhood
Awakening to lust

It's so hard to find my way home again
I don't want to find my way home again

Love, it is decisive
But love, it is no cure
Yours it was a dressing
A cloudburst good and pure

Sometimes I am not so kind
Sometimes I am a bore
And I'm not one for open
At least not anymore
It's so hard to find my way home again
I don't want to find my way home again
Unless I go with you.

SID

There's a rooster yard at Tamerlaine that's referred to as "The Frat House."

The birds inside are all too aggressive to be with the chickens, they already fight with each other enough... each rooster trying to maintain or *level up* his place in the pecking order. It gets pretty fierce in there, and one time I hurried in with Jenn, she was a caregiver at the time, to retrieve a rooster with a bloodied comb sort of cowering in a corner. Those injured roosters would wind up in the Tamerlaine hospital so that they could heal up, but the problem with that is, if they are kept away from the Frat House for too long, they could potentially be ostracized further and never be accepted again.

Tamerlaine and other sanctuaries tend to have an overabundance of roosters because male chickens are useless to the egg industry, and really, they are useless to even the most bucolic "humane" egg producers. So in addition to the many calls they get from backyard egg hobbyists who somehow wound up with a rooster where it's illegal to keep them, there are the rescue calls from people who have run across a rooster, or a few of them, who were just dumped out in a ditch somewhere to fend for themselves.

It's even worse in commercial hatcheries where the chicks are sexed immediately after they hatch and the males are sent down a conveyor belt, a sea of adorable yellow

fluffballs peeping out for their mothers, completely unaware of the fact that in seconds they will be dropped alive into a massive grinder and made into pet food.

So anyway, that's why Tamerlaine has so many roosters.

When I first started visiting the farm, I became really interested in a rooster named Sid. Sid was too aggressive to go in any of the other yards, but not aggressive enough to hold his own with the guys in the Frat House. He got bullied pretty badly, but finally discovered that he could fly just enough to get up on top of the fence and away from the fray. That went okay for a couple of days, but Sid got increasingly interested in the sexy chickens from the Tamerlaine hospital who spent their days just on the other side of the fence. They aren't very mobile, these gals. Some of them were bred to be meat, so they are way larger than a normal chicken would be. Their legs can't really handle the weight, so they have lots of issues walking and then, little Casey whose legs were so jacked up, she hung out in a wheelchair: a wheeled PVC frame with a towel clamped across it. The towel supports her weight and her legs dangle down through a couple of holes cut in the towel.

So, Sid started jumping down off of the fence and onto the backs of these hospital girls in an attempt to mount them. Which just can't happen. These chickens are pretty fragile and immobile and here's this rooster trying to jump on top of them and fuck them... So Gabrielle and Peter are faced with another problem with taking care of Sid. He can't be in any other yard but the frat house, where his only hope for surviving are his wings, But now those same wings are allowing him to endanger the hospital girls on the other side of the fence.

After much deliberation with the staff, it became apparent that the only remaining option was to clip Sid's wings, just the feathers, so that he couldn't get out of the yard anymore. Of course, this left Sid prey to the bullying of the roosters in the frat house.

As we've already determined, Sid is pretty resourceful. There's a run in the middle of the frat house—an enclosed, roofed area that provides shade on hot days, and inside is a relatively high perch, but not so high that Sid couldn't get up there with his newly clipped wings. So that's where Sid started hanging out during the day, because once he got up there, the other roosters just left him alone. And this was fine really, but at the end of the day when all the roosters went to bed in the two coops that bookend the yard, that left Sid all alone and with a choice.

Which coop full of bullying assholes do I choose for the night?

So I stood outside this fence and watched Sid dart back and forth between the two coops with a new kind of empathy I had not expected to feel for a chicken.

His instincts telling him to seek shelter for the night. Safety. But there is no safe place. Safer, but not safe.

He scurried nervously between the two coops for quite a long time. Sometimes it would look like he had made his choice. He would stop outside one of the tiny coop doors and rally for a moment and then, "no, no... not this one," and the scurrying would resume. Back and forth.

Finally, he stopped. He looked at the coop on my left, slowly inched closer to the door. He paused to summon his courage and then ran up the ladder and into the door. I heard some rustling and clucking from inside for a moment and then silence. I walked into the yard and closed the coop.

Which way do I walk home today?
Am I brave and go the normal way?
It's not so far to go around that street
It's safer there
Isn't it?

GLUE TRAP

I see you
I
I see you

When I was in middle school, my family discovered that we had a mouse problem in our house. Not a major infestation by any means, but my stepfather still decided to solve the problem using those dreadful glue traps. You know the ones, basically a small plastic pan layered with a half inch of a sticky rodent attracting substance which traps the unsuspecting creature so surely that the more he or she fights, the more hopeless the struggle because he or she just gets more stuck. Still, he or she fights until he or she dies from starvation, or dehydration, or the swift shovel of merciful human. These things are pretty grim.

I see you
I
I see you

Though I wasn't the judgemental, morally-superior vegan you see before you today, I was still quite vocal in my disapproval of these traps. But I was a kid, and my stepfather was the grown up, so I didn't have much say in the matter. As a solution, my little sister and I decided to wake up early each morning and check the traps in hopes of finding the mouse and releasing him in the field behind our house. One morning we found a mouse in the trap. We thought he had been there for a while, because even though he squirmed in panic when he first saw us, he pretty quickly stopped and then just laid there on his side breathing heavily, fully stuck to the glue. Even the side of his face was glued down.

I see you
I
I see you

Unfortunately for us, and the mouse, there was no internet in the early 80's to tell us that all we needed to do was coat his body with vegetable oil to release him, so instead we opted for a deck of playing cards. We hoped to slide the cards underneath his body to release him from the glue, and it seemed to be working at first, but once I got part of his body free, his other two feet wound up getting glued down, and then when I got those feet free again his body was back in the glue. We kept at if for a really long time, sweating in the already warm Houston sun before realizing that we were literally tearing part of the mouse's skin away from his body.

I think this was the moment that I first understood the phrase "that sinking feeling." I became all too aware that in spite of my sister's and my desperate efforts to do the right thing, we were making a hideous situation much, much worse.

I see you
I
I see you

We did finally get the mouse off of the trap, but he was so broken from our efforts and his body was so coated in glue that he didn't really move when we laid him down in the grass. We didn't know what else to do, but even though neither of us said it out loud, we knew that we had killed this mouse. Not the trap. Not our stepfather. Us.

I see you
I
I see you

I remembered this story recently because a good friend and I were talking about our relationship to animals, reincarnation, and the idea that maybe all of us who inhabit the earth are here to teach each other something, or be of service in some particular way that maybe we signed up for in a great big book.

Anyway, my friend grew up in a hunting family and she was telling me about the animals she watched suffer and die by her father's hand. This was quite devastating to her child self, but as a rather spiritually minded adult, she has developed a different perspective. She wonders if the spirits contained in those animals volunteered to show up on the earth and provide some relief to my friend and her family from the violence her father perpetrated on the humans in the house. So, by volunteering themselves to be shot, these animals were making the lives of others a little bit more tolerable. A relief valve of sorts for a violent man.

Of course, I always wonder, "but what about ME? How does THIS relate to ME?" And I remembered the animals whose lives I've seen drain away... a few of them because of my own poor judgement or just bad luck. Like the pet hamster I accidentally crushed while trying to catch him after he escaped from his cage, the little kitten I killed jumping off a swing in my backyard. I know I killed at least a turtle, a bird and one black cat with the various cars I've driven over the years. Of course. The little mouse on the glue trap, killed by the shadow side of my desire to liberate. Were they here to teach me, too? Were they feeding the compassion that has become my sometimes over-the-top veganism? Or maybe theirs are the voices that shut me up when I realize I am becoming too much.

This leads me, of course, deeper into me. What did I sign up for in that big book of reincarnation vocations? Am I defending animals? Spreading universal empathy through incessant Facebook posts? Could it be that the entire universe is counting on me to show humanity how to act right?

Or maybe I'm just dust.

MILK

Last night I visited a "humane" dairy farm. It was sad to see the looks on the grazing cows that seemed to say, "can you get us out of here?" It was sad to say goodbye again and again to the cow who followed me through the pasture as far as she could go without hitting the electric fence. It was sad to see the cow who slipped on a puddle of her own piss and fell to her knees on the cement floor of the milking room. It was sad to see the cow who tried to resist going into the milking chamber only to be slapped and pushed by the human who worked there until she gave up. It was sad to see the cows lined up in the chamber with mechanical pumps attached to their bodies that sometimes malfunctioned and made frightening noises before falling to the floor and getting tangled in their feet.

It was saddest of all to see the room of baby calves separated from their mothers and alone in single stalls, some no more than a month old, so desperate to nurse that they stretched their necks out as far as they could to suck on my jeans, or my fingers, or my camera strap, or my elbow, or whatever else they could reach. Their innocent eyes were panicked and confused.

It was an incredibly sad place.

Dairy is sad.

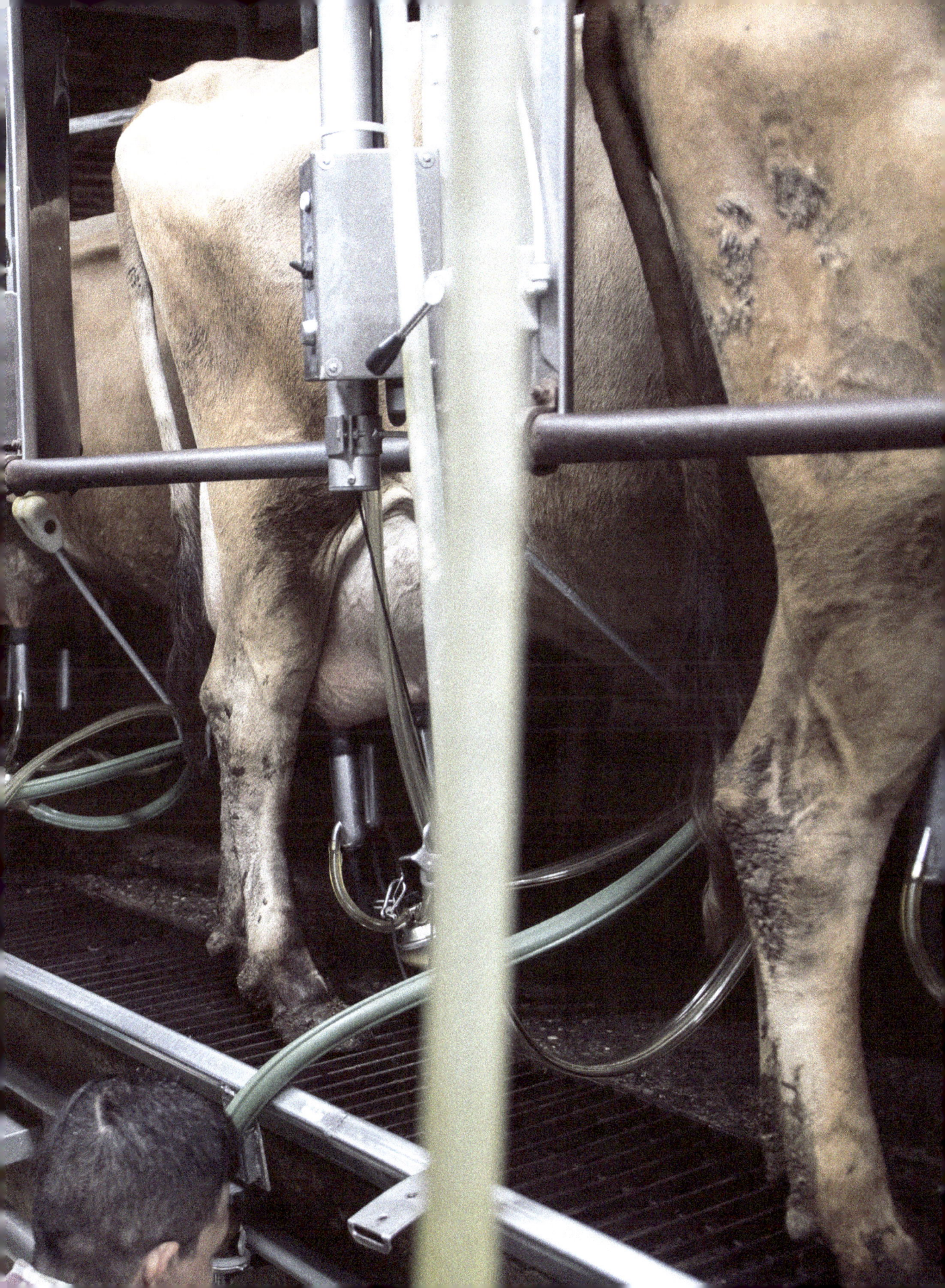

CLARA

A lot of animals scare me.

While prepping to run my first 200 mile relay race through Cape Cod with the Strong Hearts Vegan Power running team, it dawned on me that I would likely be running at night. In the dark. On a highway. With no one around and lit only by the moon and my headlamp, which of course had the potential to electrocute and kill me if it was raining. When the reality of this nighttime run hit, I began to run down the list of wild animals I would surely encounter. I was able to rule out lions and tigers pretty easily, same for alligators and enraged chimpanzees, and for some reason I didn't even think about snakes which are honestly a possibility even here on this stage when you think about it. I mean they climb up through toilets for christ' sake. I settled on bears and began to obsess on what I would do when (not if) I encountered one, and what would be the most veganic way of handling it.

This is how I think: *what is the worst possible thing that can happen and you better watch out for it cus I am sure as fuck not going down like that.* I cultivate this kind of fear thinking too. For a long time I was obsessed with the tv show *I Survived* on the Biography Channel. I would watch it late at night, listening to survivors of near death experiences tell stories of how they almost died. It could be anything from a kidnapping, to getting acid thrown in your face by your new boyfriend's ex-girlfriend, to getting your arm caught in farm equipment and having to saw it off with a rusty pocket knife before you are pulled into its screeching gears. One girl got pinned under the rubble of her house during a tornado and laid there "screaming, screaming, SCREAMING" from the pain before she got rescued.

Oh, and bears. I remember distinctly two survivors of bear attacks. My favorite one to be freaked out by was a guy who took his dog out to pee in the country somewhere, just in his driveway, and there was a fucking bear who was obviously pissed about something so grabbed the guy and started kicking his ass. The part of the story that I remember the most vividly was his description of the bear's teeth scraping against his skull. He survived—hideously scarred—but he lived to tell the tale and freak my shit out probably for the rest of my life.

One morning at the farm, just as I was getting my bearings with this whole, "being outside and sweating a lot" thing, Maggie gazes out the window, cradling her coffee cup and croons,

"Oh, I forgot to tell you guys. I saw a little bear by the compost yesterday."

I nearly leapt out my skin, because I had been to that very compost pile numerous times the previous day, not knowing that there had been an actual bear sighting.

"Oh?" I said as calmly as I could, "what did you do?"

"I just stood there for a while and watched him."

"Were you inside?"

"No, I was just standing a few hundred yards away from him."

Didn't she know that the number one rule when dealing with bears was not to get between a mama bear and her cub? WHERE WAS THE MAMA BEAR!? And that's the problem, if you do what any sane person would do in this situation and hightail it out of there, there's always the possibility that your path could take you between the cub and his mother and then... you're fucked.

If you are thinking that this is all leading up to a story of my own encounter with a bear, I am sorry to disappoint you, but you are incorrect. This story is about a creature who is equally, if not more, terrifying:

Clara the pig.

Clara is a feisty, stubborn, two-hundred some odd pound pig who lives at Tamerlaine Farm. Before I get too deep in describing to you what an asshole I find her to be, I do feel that I owe it to her to give you some of her background. Clara was rescued from a hoarding situation. She lived with a couple who had way too many animals. The hoarding husband passed away, leaving the hoarding wife alone and overwhelmed. All of the animals fell into various states of neglect, including Clara, who was rescued from the bathroom where she had apparently lived for many years.

So maybe I'm the asshole here for not being more understanding of Clara and her... issues.

There was one weekend in particular that I learned these animals didn't give a rats ass that I planned to make performance art about shoveling their shit. The boys in the frat house encircled me and started pecking, flapping, and kicking at my legs until I ran screaming from their yard. Then, the cute little *bantam* roosters demonstrated that they could jump above the tops of my work boots and bite the shit out of my kneecaps when I was only trying to fill up their goddamned water. This was also the weekend that Clara bit me. I stood too close to her when she was eating and she casually turned

her head and bit the fuck out of my leg and then went right back to eating as if nothing had happened.

I did eventually get comfortable around the roosters again, but It was several months before I returned to Clara's yard. Peter and Gabrielle were briefing me one morning on what they needed my help with, and almost as if she thought she could sneak it by me Gabby said,

"And then you and Peter will deep clean the pig barn."

She must have seen the blood rush out of my face because she immediately added details about how the pigs would not be in the yard and we could just close the gate so I wouldn't have to worry about Clara. Fine.

So Peter and I went to work on the clean up, and you best believe I had one eye on that gate at all times. Clara and the other two pigs, Artie and Ferdinand, were nowhere to be seen. It was fall and they loved eating the acorns that were scattered around the property. After we worked for a while, Peter had to run up to the house, so I stayed, enclosed in the yard clearing hay out of the barn with a pitchfork.

No more than two minutes after Peter was out of sight, I heard a familiar sound: Clara's aggressive snort.

I peered through the window of the barn, and there was Clara staring dead at me. She had obviously been lurking, waiting for the perfect moment to come and terrorize me. I swear I could see it in her face.

"Just act natural and keep working. She'll go away," I thought to myself as I realized that the wheelbarrow was pretty full and I was going to have to make a trip through that gate, past Clara and over to the compost where that fucking bear hangs out.

I gave it a few minutes to see if Peter would return, looking at my phone to kill the time, and maybe give Clara the impression that I was busy working on something. She didn't buy it, and neither did my phone. No signal out in the country and I was too far from the house to connect to the wifi.

Fuck.

That left me trapped in a pig pen by a pig who was still staring me down. So, I started sizing her up.

She has hooves. I have thumbs! She walks on four legs and I only have two but I also have arms and hands. Oh, and I have a mouth too, but hers is bigger and way gnarlier. I'm pretty sure she can run as fast as me and I really don't want Peter to come back to find me running in terror from a pig anyway, so that's not really an option.

No matter what, I am the fucking human here and I'm supposed to have the upper hand. So get it together Harren! Are you going to let this pig scare you into standing here all day? If you get through this, imagine what other fears you can overcome in your life. DO IT! JUST DO IT! MAKE YOUR DREAMS COME TRUE! Yesterday, you said tomorrow so JUST DO IT!

Clara interrupted my inner motivational speech with another insistent sort, to which I responded with another terrified shriek.

Am I going to let this pig get the best of me? No. I have a plan.

I positioned the wheelbarrow between me and the gate, thinking that when I open the gate—from *behind* the wheelbarrow—it will serve as my shield should Clara decide to attack. Clara will walk in, and I will breeze out behind her. No problem.

I took a deep breath, reached over the wheelbarrow and unlatched the gate. It slowly swung open and Clara sassily sauntered a few steps and then very deliberately stopped. Blocking my exit. I'm not kidding. Clara was now officially fucking with me.

"Okay, Clara... go on in."

It was a stand-off. Either she would move, or I'd be stuck there until Peter got back, hiding behind a pissy hay and shit-filled wheelbarrow.

I still had the wheelbarrow between me and Clara so I gently used it to try to nudge her into motion. She ignored me a couple of times and then, that bitch, lunged at me. Like a total wuss, I jumped back and screamed as she continued her constitutional into her domain. Clara 2. Michael zero.

Even though things didn't unfold exactly as I had planned, I was pleased that Clara was out of my way and apparently tired of toying with me. Relieved, I grabbed ahold of the wheelbarrow and started heading over to the compost... where that fucking bear hangs out.

THEIR EYES

Midway through my Summer 2017 tour with The Animal Show, I found myself outside Farmer John's Slaughterhouse with Los Angeles Animal Save. The organization is part of The Save Movement, which is comprised of groups around the world who bear witness to farmed animals on their way to slaughter. This was my second visit to a slaughterhouse that day. The first was in the early evening in an industrial area where I had arrived after the cows had been dropped off. I could see them in the distance, standing in a large pen all alone, without any access to food or water that I could see. They would wait there through the night and be slaughtered in the morning.

When I arrived at Farmer John's just before midnight, I was really surprised by the turn out of activists. There were maybe 75 people preparing for the vigil. The group was busy, well organized, and deeply reverent. Cases of water bottles were stacked on the sidewalk, some opened to fill sprayers with water. Activists greeted one another solemnly with quiet, soulful embraces. Two images were being projected on the building, one was a video with guidelines for activists on how the vigil would be conducted, and the other was a simple statement projected high on the wall of what might have been the actual slaughterhouse:

"Please stop!
I'm begging you!
I want to live!
—The Animals"

PLEASE STOP!
I'M BEGGING YOU!
I WANT TO LIVE!

-THE ANIMALS

STOP CRUELTY - GO VEGAN

@THESAVEMOVEMENT

NO LOITERING
OR TRESPASSING
PRIVATE PARKING
FARMER JOHN
EMPLOYEES ONLY

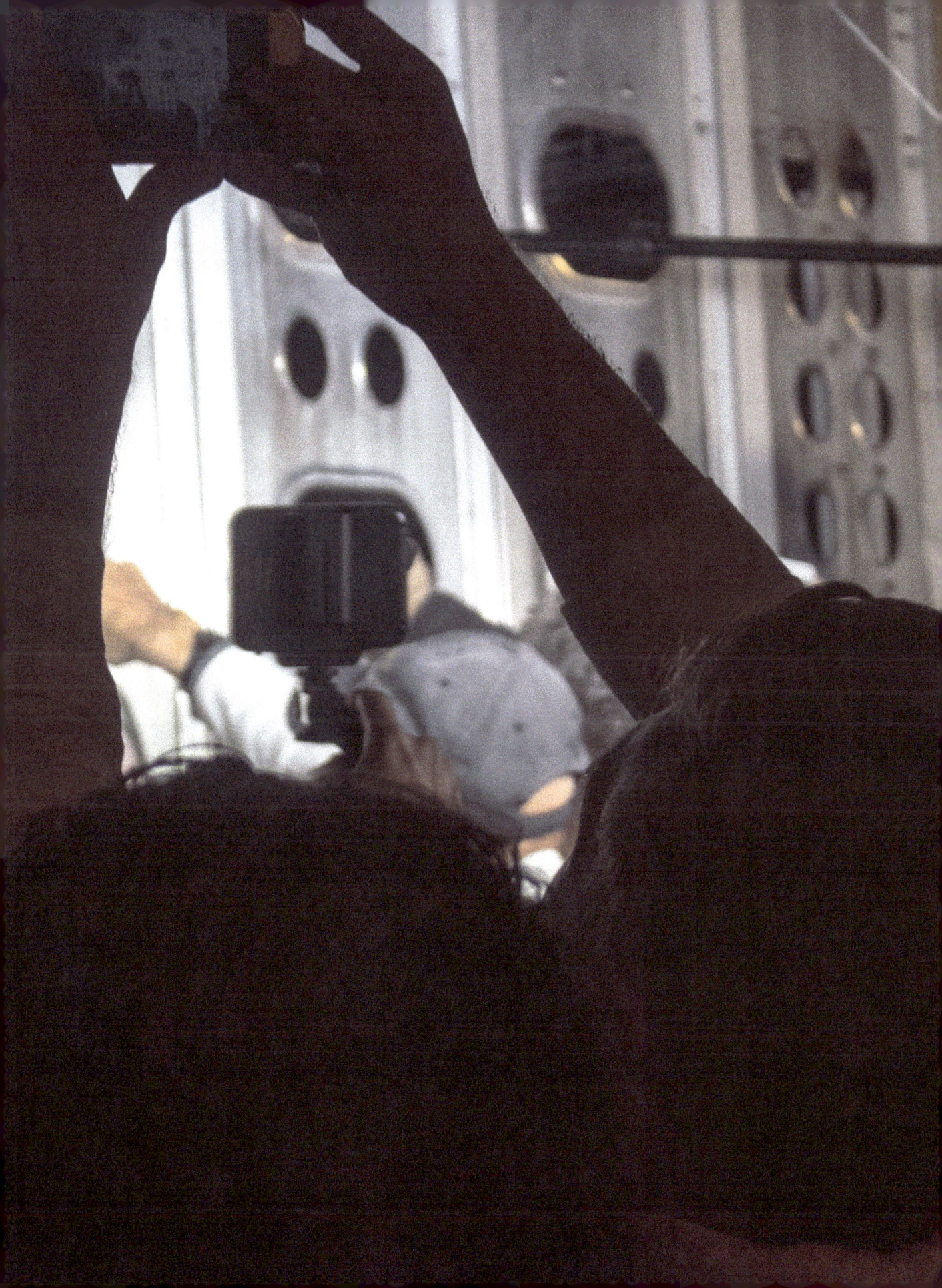

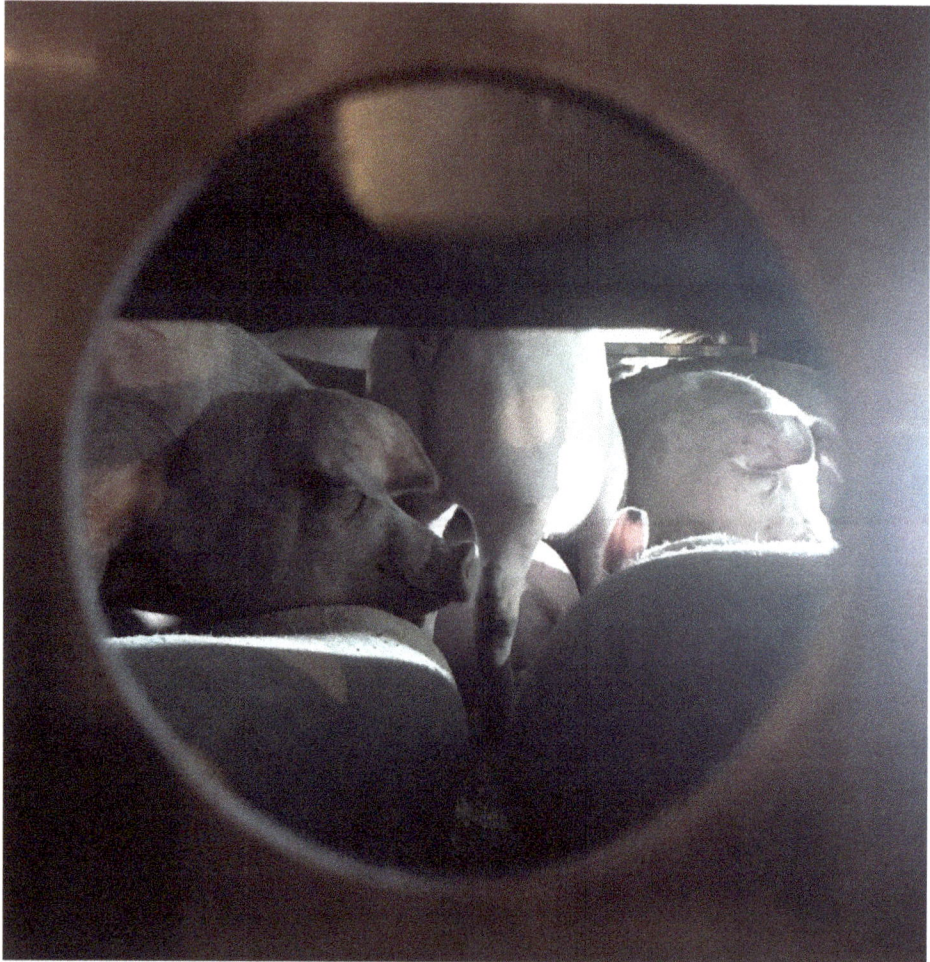

The first truck arrived around 12:20 AM. The eighteen wheeler pulled up slowly to where we were stationed in silence. The group approached the truck. Water bottles were opened and offered to the pigs through the ventilation holes in the sides of the truck. Other people held large sprayers which were pumped to send streams of water through the holes at the top of the truck. Another group of activists lit the inside of the truck with LED lights on long telescopic poles. I stayed back and took photographs and video in the interest of documenting the vigil, but more so out of fear of what I would see inside those trucks.

Over time, though, my fear was overshadowed by my desire to be of some comfort to the souls in the trucks. I grabbed two bottles of water, opened one and put the other in the roomy pocket of my shorts. I stood in silence with the crowd until the next truck arrived, slowly easing up in front of us. Seemingly as one unit, we approached the truck, and for the first time I heard up close the whispers of the others:

"I'm sorry this is happening to you."
"I love you."
"You matter."

I could barely discern the whispers from the sidewalk, but from the crowd, I could hear it all. Humans trying to find comfort for these animals. I worked hard to choke back my tears as I peered through the ventilation holes of the truck, searching for a pig who was conscious enough to accept my offering of water. The pigs were jammed tightly together, some had visible bloody scrapes on their sides, but none had space to turn around, though some were laying, half-conscious on the ground. Most of the pigs who were conscious stared blankly, but I located one close to me who seemed to be responding.

"Do you want some water?" I asked as I cautiously reached my open water bottle into the truck. I let a little water drip onto the top of her snout so she would know it was water, and she immediately began gulping the water from the bottle, quickly and desperately. As she drank I retrieved my second bottle from my pocket and screwed off the top with my teeth, just in time to replace the now empty bottle of water. She took the new bottle just like she did the first, gulping down the precious water.

"Does anyone have another bottle? I need more water!" I whispered desperately as the second bottle neared empty.

"Here," someone replied, handing me an open but full bottle of water which I quickly offered to the dehydrated pig inside.

She was drinking more slowly now, and the calmness gave me the resolve to observe more carefully the other pigs. Most of them remained lethargic, some even dripped foam from their mouths as they stared absently ahead. The most devastating thing to see, though, were their eyes. I had never witnessed such despair and absolute terror on a fellow earthling as I did in that truck.

As the pig in the truck finished the third bottle of water, I heard a fellow activist shout,"Back up! Step away from the truck! Only sprayers!"

The entire crowd stepped back solemnly, leaving only those with sprayers, who sent streams of water into the mouths of the pigs who desperately tried to drink through the ventilation holes. The truck shifted into gear, lurched into motion, and turned left into the driveway of the slaughterhouse.

Tears streaming, I stood and waited for the next truck.

KAPOROS

Each year 60,000 chickens descend on Brooklyn for Yom Kippur.

They don't transport themselves, of course, because chickens can't fly and, as far as I know, they don't observe Yom Kippur either. In spite of this, they attend the pre-game Yom Kippur ritual known as Kaporos in great numbers. These chickens are the most important guests, and arguably pay the greatest price for admission. Practitioners of this ritual grasp a chicken, pinning her wings behind her back. They raise the chicken above their heads and wave her around three times while reciting the prayer:

This is my exchange,
this is my substitute,
this is my atonement.
This chicken will go to its death,
while I will enter and proceed
to a good long life and to peace.

The Rabbi then hands the chicken to the executioner who slits the chicken's throat, tosses her into a bucket and lets her bleed out. She waits there for as long as it takes to die.

זב חליפתי, זה
תמורתי,זהכפרתי,
זה התרנגול ילך
למיטה ואני אלך
לחיים טובים
ארוכים ולשלום.

Peace.

You can hear the chickens cries of pain for blocks around the ritual site. It's the only thing striking enough to distract from the smell of death and blood in the street. They say that the birds sing out of happiness during the ritual. It doesn't take a genius, though, to see that these chickens do not know joy and probably never have.

* * *

The night before the Kaporos rituals began, I rode around the Hasidic neighborhoods of Boro Park and Williamsburg with a few friends who had haphazardly decided to attempt a rescue. I was nervous, but the excitement of saving even a few lives pushed me along. The four of us drove around in an SUV for several hours in the middle of the night. To my surprise there were others out too: trucks stacked with crates of live chickens. Each crate held about twelve chickens and was made of what once was brightly colored plastic, now dingy grey and white, covered in shit from the imprisoned birds.

We were out there for a long time, looking at potential targets. I began to wonder if the trucks were still making deliveries when we finally came across one. I had been picturing a U-Haul truck at most. Something small but utilitarian. What we saw then, though, was no U-Haul. It was a big 18 wheeler, stopped in the middle of the street. There were hundreds of these crates stacked on the truck, each crate full of chickens who were crying out in what sounded like panic. I wondered if they were crying out for help, but in retrospect, I realize they probably had no idea what "help" was. All they probably knew was the inside of a shed and now these crates and this truck. Their only experience had been suffering and fear.

There appeared to be four men on the truck who tossed the live chicken-stuffed crates onto the street. I heard them shouting over the diesel engine. And, of course, the sounds of the birds crying out as their crates were tossed from ten feet or so onto the pavement. Hard.

We sat in our vehicle staring at the scene in silence. I can still taste the crushing helplessness—that sinking feeling—that enveloped the four of us when we saw that truck. There were so many.

So many voices.

It's now three AM. All the deliveries appear to have been made and if we don't act

fast, we will miss our chance to save any chickens. We've decided on our target. Right out on the street, literally in the street where one might park a car, there are 30 or so of these crates full of chickens stacked up. There's no one around. This is it. The two of us in the backseat hop out and run over to the chickens and I realize I'm wearing these fucking bright green pants. I didn't know this was even going to be happening tonight but it is and I'm almost there. I grab a crate as our lookout opens the back door of the SUV. I toss the crate inside and turn back for another just in time to see my compatriot returning from the stack.

"Wegottagowegottagowegottagowegottago," he whispers.

I don't see what's happening but I run like hell and we all jump in the truck and just as my door closes I hear a SMACK and through the window I see four hasidic men screaming at us. One has a huge piece of plywood and he is beating on our truck. The others beat with their fists, and they are all screaming at us: "FUCK YOU FUCK YOU FUCK YOU THIEVES!"

Our driver speeds off and we get the fuck out of there.

As we drove, I took a peek in the back of the truck to look at our rescues. At first glance, the chickens in the crate appeared to be in decent condition. I mean they

were covered in shit and there were bald spots in their feathers from all the rough handling, but everyone appeared to be alive and conscious. But... they were *babies*, still peeping and small with fuzz instead of feathers on their backs. They're the same age as the ones I used to buy in pieces at the grocery store. They seemed like objects there, ingredients, but here they are all in one piece. Individuals in need.

* * *

When I showed up the first night of protests, there was only a small group of activists on the scene, but it was still early. The people who had arrived before me explained that at this particular spot, they had moved the ritual indoors. There was rumoured to be a small location where chickens were being sold on a residential street in Boro Park, Brooklyn so a few of us headed over there to protest. We had to park several blocks from the site, but even from that distance, the stench hit my face immediately upon getting out of the car.

"Is that the chickens?" I could hear their cries in the distance and the smell got worse with each step. It was horrific.

Then we saw the site, a dump of a place on a corner lot, half enclosed by a chain link fence. There were stacks of the now familiar crates on the pavement. Some contained live chickens but there were quite a few whose occupants had already been slaughtered. A rabbi wearing a blood soaked apron held a crying chicken by her wings and waved her over a baby in a stroller, handed the chicken over to another man who jerked the chicken's head back, slit her throat, and tossed her twitching body into a trash can. Until that moment... seeing the ritual take place for the first time, I had, on some level, believed that they weren't really doing that. Were they?

And I'm not exaggerating, the smell was overwhelming and I wanted to puke when I looked down and saw that I was standing in a river of unknown liquid whose source could not be seen behind the tarped off back end of the lot. The putrid liquid was running down the driveway and into the street. We stood in silence watching the scene. Smelling the smells. Hearing the cries and ignoring the proprietor who was taunting us. I guess he felt safe and unthreatened by the five sign-wielding hippies standing in his driveway looking sad and taking pictures.

But one by one, our numbers grew. When there were ten of us, we created a picket line, marching and shouting on this little residential street. It was well past 9 PM and some of the neighbors started coming outside. Then there were 15 of us, and then 20. The proprietor had begun to change his tune and was starting to look nervous. He actually offered one of us a live chicken or two in hopes that it would get us to go away, but now there were 25 of us and we weren't leaving.

Then the police arrived in two cruisers and a big van. The cops opened the back doors of the van and dragged out barricades and set them up for us across the street. At first we were getting very "hell no, we won't go" about the whole thing until a few of us looked around and realized that we were surrounded on all sides by the residents of this Orthodox neighborhood. They had come out of their homes to see what the hubbub was about. We were far outnumbered, but energized by the fact that our still small group had been able to create such a disturbance. At some point soon after the cops arrived, I started to hear car alarms going off. One after another. Some residents decided to drown us out by triggering their alarms. Picture it, 30 some-odd shouting protesters with signs, two streets blocked off and crowded with jeering Orthodox Jews, three police vehicles with flashing lights, and the echoes of car alarms in the streets of a residential neighborhood in Brooklyn, New York.

And then I saw something that changed everything. One of the men who was standing in front of the entrance to the ritual site had grabbed a live chicken and began thrashing her over his head to torment us. He was torturing this chicken to get back at us.

Our chants almost immediately changed with the energy of helplessness I assume we all felt. We were angry before. Now we chanted solemnly:

We see you.
We care.
We're sorry.
We're trying.

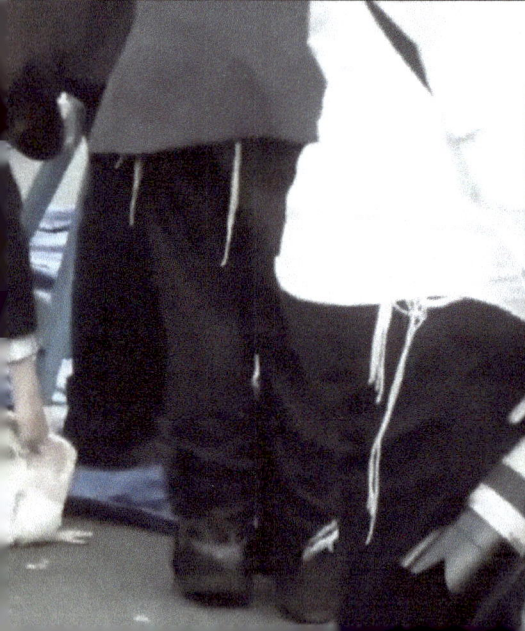

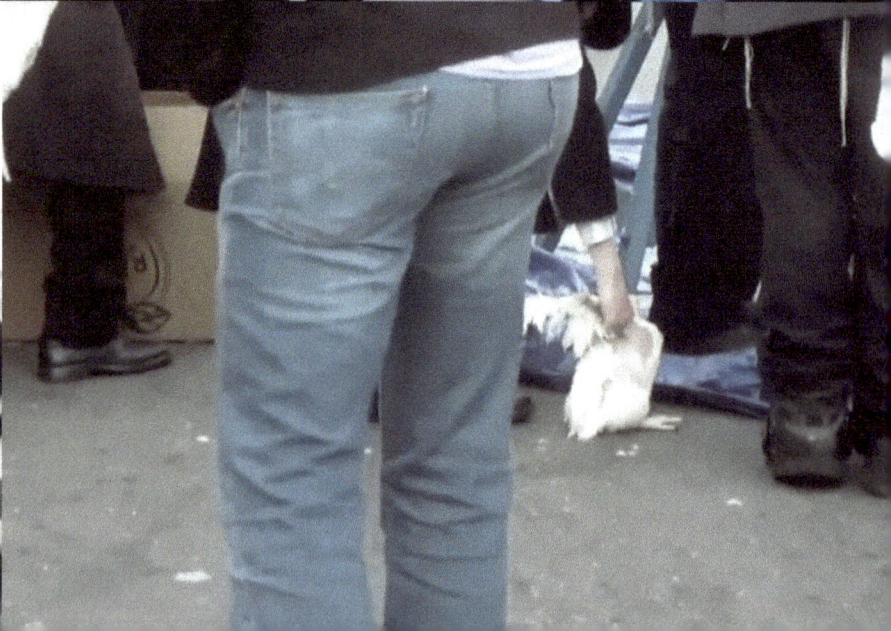

BLOOD AND BEAKS

I spent a great deal of time this week protesting the religious ritual of Kaporos in Brooklyn. For those who do not know, in this ritual, some ultra-Orthodox Jewish people swing a live chicken over their head three times by her wings while saying a prayer, then slit the chicken's throat and literally throw the dying animal into a garbage can. Multiply this by approx 60,000 chickens and you can imagine the horror on the street. The practitioners claim they donate the dead bodies to charity but my activist friends have collected a tremendous amount of video and photographs that prove otherwise.

Wednesday night, I stood next to my friend Ethan at one of the ritual sites. Noticing a pile of black garbage bags on the street, I asked Ethan if he agreed that they might be filled with dead chickens. I felt one of the bags and then began tearing them open. To my horror each of these 15 or so bags was full of decaying bodies of chickens. I lost my mind. I began screaming at the men standing around jeering at us and mocking us for trying to stand up for these innocents. I don't remember what I said but whatever it was shut them up and they looked at me as if I had gone insane. I kept screaming. After attempting in vain to make a report to two separate police officers about this blatant violation of the law (decaying animal bodies and blood on the street), I walked up and down the street screaming at the Orthodox residents of the neighborhood, "There are dead bodies in those bags! Your community is lying to you!"

Since that moment I have been asking myself why this ritual enrages me so much when it is really no worse than the many, many other forms of animal abuse that are normalized in our society. I think I am beginning to understand. Showing up at these protests and witnessing this abject suffering and torture is traumatizing. Everywhere I turn there are live chickens dying in crates from the heat, starvation, dehydration, or injuries they sustained during transport. There are people walking around carrying screaming chickens by their wings, and the smell of death and rotting everywhere.

At the same time there are people defending this treatment of the animals. They surround us. They spit at us. They call us nazis, morons, and idiots. They demand to know what kind of shoes we are wearing, what we ate for breakfast, why we don't get a job, what about zebras being eaten by lions, plants have feelings too, we've been doing this for thousands of years... all the same bullshit reasons meat, dairy, and egg eaters give about their abusive habits.

This week of Kaporos is a magnification of my day to day life. I am surrounded by otherwise compassionate people who participate gleefully in animal abuse and whom I desperately beg to have mercy on their victims. People get angry at me on the daily for suggesting they make another choice than to participate in animal slaughter and abuse. People act as if I am being unreasonable when I mention that I don't want to see people I love consuming dead animal bodies. People defend their choice to abuse animals three time a day with the same illogical arguments that I heard at these protests.

I will continue to protest Kaporos, but I will no longer be focusing my anger only on this community. What they are doing is no worse that any other form of violence against animals I watch my family and friends participate in daily. Your chicken sandwich, your eggs, your milk, your hamburger, your leather shoes— all the same abject suffering I saw at the Kaporos rituals this week. You may be able to pretend that the flesh on your plate was not once a tormented, suffering individual who wanted to escape, who wanted freedom, who wanted to live... but I cannot. Not any more. And I can no longer be polite when I see you taking pleasure in their suffering. It is just as blatantly cruel and unnecessary as that ritual I was protesting this week. Think about it.

Stop torturing animals. Today. It's well past time and there is no reason to continue. Stop. Just stop.

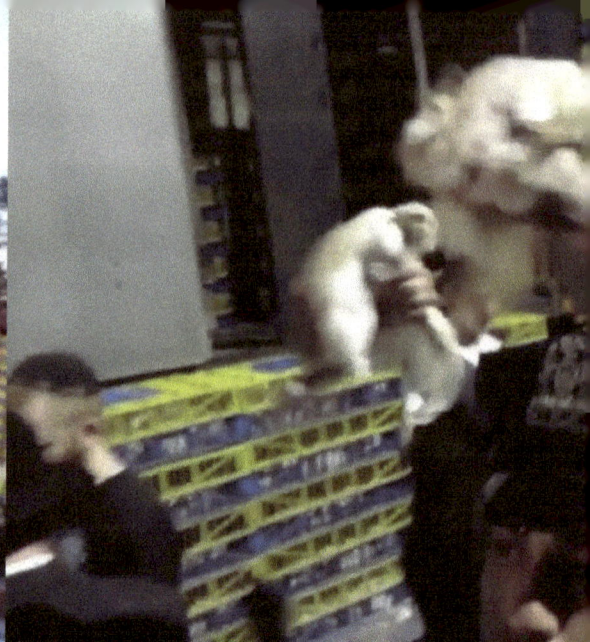

DISEMBODIED VOICE OF HEAVEN

DVOH - Michael.

silence

DVOH - Michael.

MICHAEL - WHAT?

DVOH - That's too much now, Michael.

MICHAEL - No. They're not listening. They have to listen. They're still killing.

DVOH - They won't listen to that anymore, Michael.

MICHAEL - So I should just give up? Let this just go on? I can't stand seeing it anymore.

DVOH - Michael.

silence

DVOH - Michael.

MICHAEL - Fuck. What?

DVOH - Don't give up, Michael.

MICHAEL - They're not listening. They don't care.

DVOH - They care, Michael. Look in front of you. They're listening.

MICHAEL - I don't see them.

DVOH - Look harder. They're right in front of you, Michael.

MICHAEL - (shifting) Oh. Them.

DVOH - Yes. There's another way.v

MICHAEL - Um. Twitter?

DVOH - No, Michael. Tell them the truth.

MICHAEL - I just...

DVOH - All of it. Tell them all of it, Michael.

THE POEM

There was a day
After I put down the bottle
And the pills, and the tiny squares of hallucinogen soaked paper
The car key my boyfriend dipped in a tiny little baggy
"I thought you brought me in this bathroom stall to make out but..."
"Okay"
Sniff
"yeah"
Sniff
It was six years after that
And I was putting it down and picking me up for the first time.

They told me I needed a higher power but I never knew a gay boy like me was allowed
That he could be
That I could be loved or divine

I wanted to come to believe but I didn't know in whom

So I read and I prayed like a mechanical arm diving and dipping into the cheap

Toys and stickers and keychains

I read Buddha and natives and Wiccans and pagans and New Agers and I sought my god so hard because I wanted and needed and hungered to fill that God-shaped hole inside me until one day I heard

"Listen"
"Listen"

So I started to and you know what I heard?

That small voice asked me what I saw. What was the same with the Buddha and natives and Wiccans and pagans and New Agers and...

It's that we are all one.
One.

Do unto others because they are you and you are they and there is no separation. But it's never easy because the way we see is separation and that's how we think we survive and protect these tiny raw hearts that
only
want
to breathe

And I began to breathe and take in trees and rocks and and I cleaned up wreckage and started finding a way to be whole like I never had been before.

We are all one.

As I get older it's not so easy to live in wonder—to let my sopping heart beat plainly in one outstretched hand. It finds its way out and up when I stop paying attention but then I see and remember and forget.

But there are things I cannot forget,

That render my chest crystalline and frail

When I first met Clara, the pig-headed pig

I could not stop seeing what they do

What I did with every bite

I didn't have to close my eyes to see her

Hanging by her legs, hanging by the billions

Shrieking, screaming for mercy over the

Lives of her sisters, *my* sisters leaking crimson to the floor

The blood-soaked apron of my brother on the kill line

His single blade

Slits

One thrashing throat

Every

Five

Seconds

And she just wanted to eat in peace.

I see your plate and I grieve
For lives I never got to know
Lives I learned only with my tongue
Lives that wanted to be alive

If we are all one, then aren't we *all* one?
And if we are all one then why?
Why do you take a life you claim to love?
And why are *you* sitting, seething in your seat
Asking who I am to judge your choice to kill

You know the truth

I told you—

Your burger, your shoes, your milk, your eggs

All the same suffering I saw on those Orthodox streets

We are responsible even for what we refuse to see.

We are to blame and we all have a choice

Compassion has placed its roots

At the base of your soul and

All you have to do is let go

Allow it, and it will find its way

Up your spine

Free it.

It will be your guide.

I had my day of awakening

When the fuck are you having yours?

TILLY

It's a chilly November morning. My favorite. I'm heading out to see a new friend who I haven't seen in a few weeks. Tilly the chicken. I was the first to lift Tilly from his crate when he was rescued from Kaporos. Probably the first gentle human hands he felt in his life. Tilly's legs were badly splayed when I picked him up and he was of course in terrible condition, dehydrated and starving. When I first met him, I wondered if he would live.

But now I approach his yard at his new home and I see two chickens running towards me. It's Tilly and his new best friend, Lefty, hobbling behind him, still wounded from his past life.

In the grass. In the sun. Tilly is running to greet me.

They both seem to smile at me, and though I have no idea if Tilly remembers me, I think he does. I squat down in the grass and he hops up on my legs, and tucks his head under my arm.

In only a few weeks, like many chickens rescued from these horrific scenes, Tilly will die. Though he looks healthier now than when I first met him, his system is frail from abuse and neglect. When I hear about his death I will wonder if it was worth it. Was it worth risking my own safety and freedom for Tilly to have just a few more weeks to live?

But now I am sitting in this yard in the sun, a chilly breeze rustles his feathers and the leaves on the ground. I am loving this chicken and he is loving me.

I cannot know what any of this really means, but I know that this moment right here?

It matters.

WRITTEN & PERFORMED BY
MICHAEL HARREN'S

THE ANIMAL SHOW
SUMMER 20 TOUR 17

JULY 9   HOUSTON, TX   THE REC
JULY 26   LOS ANGELES, CA   BOOTLE
JULY 30   BERKELEY, CA   BERKEL
AUGUST 14   PORTLAND, OR   TABOR

MICHAELHARREN.COM

PERFORMANCE HISTORY AND CREDITS

4 APRIL 2014

"Glue Trap" at The Parkside Lounge, New York City

New Work New York curated by Gardiner Comfort

Michael Harren - Synthesizer, Electronics, and Voice

10 JANUARY 2016

"Corky" at BADYHouse Storytelling Concert, Brooklyn, New York

Curated by Robin Bady

Michael Harren - Voice

28 APRIL 2016

The Animal Show (in-progress reading) at Judson Memorial Church, New York City

Directed by Adam Fitzgerald

Michael Harren - Synthesizer, Electronics, and Voice

27, 28, AND 29 OCTOBER 2016

The Animal Show at Dixon Place, New York City

Directed by Adam Fitzgerald

Michael Harren - Piano, Synthesizer, Electronics, and Voice

David Packer - Viola

Lea Coloff - Cello

30 JULY 2017

The Animal Show at Berkeley Animal Rights Center, Berkeley, California

Directed by Adam Fitzgerald

Michael Harren - Synthesizer, Electronics, and Voice

Viola - Ben Richard

14 AUGUST 2017

The Animal Show at Taborspace, Portland, Oregon
Directed by Adam Fitzgerald
Michael Harren - Piano, Synthesizer, Electronics, and Voice

22 OCTOBER 2017

"Their Eyes" at Symphony Space, New York City
Compassion Arts & Culture and Animals Festival
Michael Harren - Piano, Synthesizer, Electronics, and Voice
Violins - Brian Ford & Brian Thompson
Viola - Karen Waltuch
Cello - Anastasia Golenishcheva

8 & 9 NOVEMBER 2017

The Animal Show at Dixon Place, New York City
Directed by Adam Fitzgerald
Michael Harren - Piano, Synthesizer, Electronics, and Voice
Violins - Brian Ford & Brian Thompson
Viola - Karen Waltuch
Cello - Anastasia Golenishcheva

16 NOVEMBER 2017

The Animal Show at The Rotunda, Philadelphia, Pennsylvania

Directed by Adam Fitzgerald

Michael Harren - Piano, Synthesizer, Electronics, and Voice

Violins - Brian Ford & Brian Thompson

Viola - Karen Waltuch

27 JANUARY 2018

The Animal Show at The Rochester Vegan Community Center Rochester, New York

Directed by Adam Fitzgerald

Michael Harren - Synthesizer, Electronics, and Voice

SPECIAL THANKS

Adam Fitzgerald, luke kurtis, Peter Nussbaum, Gabrielle Stubbert, Diana Bezanski, Micah Bucey, Judson Memorial Church, Blake Drummond, Izzy Jacobus, Marc S. Wood, Jill Carnegie, Vegans of New York, Dixon Place, James T. Lane, Ben Strothmann, Steven Klapow, Ethan Ciment, Michael Suchman, David Cabrera, Alexander Grey, Catherine and Dan Barufaldi, Mariann Sullivan, Jasmin Singer, Martin Rowe, Melanie Hiller, Rina Deych... and my beautiful animal rights activist community in NYC.

This project was co-created with the members of my Patreon community. This book and accompanying album would not have been possible without the ongoing support of:

Younique Abilities, Stacy Adkins, Joan Albert, Gregory Alexander, Sara Andrews, Jo Anna, Sam Armstrong, Joy Askew, Catherine and Dan Barufadli, Eve Beglarian, Candace Bell, Edita Birnkrant, RJ Broaddus, Matt Burlingame, Joel Capolongo, Joel Capolongo, Jill Carnegie, Rochelle Carter, Maddie Cartwright, Melissa Centoni, Collin Cherry, Robert Conroy, Catherine Craig, Eban Crawford, Fiona Creedy, Jenny Cruise, Melyssa Davis, Michael Deavers, Andrew DellaPietra, Antoine Dixon, Wendy Edwards, Electric Shoebox Studios, Andy English, Corey Evatt, The Evidence Box, Kate Fermoile, JL Fields, Tere Fox, Jenn Friedman, Kate Froio, Shelley Frost, Rachel McCrystal and John Frusciante, Katy Fulfer, Joël Galeran, Liz Dee and Nick Garin, Liz Garrett, Carmella and Carlo Giardina, Jimie Gibbon, Brett Gleason, Peter Guarino, Lee

Hall, Michelle Harris, Tiffany and Steph Harris, Abigail Hastings, Timothy Hazekamp, Ren Hurst, Izzy Jacobus, Daniel Lee James, Valancy Jane, Laurie Johnston, Rachel Kay, Francesca Kennedy, Laura Kline, David Koropkin, Victoria Koulouris, Tara Krostad, Marty Krutolow, luke kurtis, Shawna Laemlein, Natalie LaGuerrier, Kristin Lajeunesse, Paul Langevin, Samantha Leblanc, Vance Lehmkuhl, Wendy Linton, Jaylene Lopez, Britt LoSacco, Hana Low, Penelope Low, Walker Lukens, Emmett Jack Lundberg, Nate Maingard, Peter Marino, Donald Matteson, Bobby McCullough, Andy Melton, Eric Milano, Camden Miller, Donny Moss, Daaimah Mubashir, Sean Murphy, Kane Nash, Nicole Nelson, Gabrielle Stubbert and Peter Nussbaum, Jane O'Hara, Stacy Owens, Chris Palmieri, Jessica Patiño, Liza Pavelich, Brandon Peters, Marcus Pingel, Paul Point, Andrea Powell, Melissa Ratisher, Daniel and Beth Lily Redwood, Gina Renzi, Cindee Rifkin, Jeremy Ritz, Jamie Robinson, Bess Rogers, Abra Rosen, Piper Hoffman and Aviv Roth, Rachel Roth, Celene Ryan, Jessica Ryle, Nathan Semmel and Meredeth Schriver, Tamera Siler, Laurence Simon, Shana Starman, Ben Strothmann, Ethan Ciment and Michael Suchman, Eddie Sullivan, Mariann Sullivan, Daniel Sweeney, Evan Tasch, Jon Tedd, Carla Athena Tejada, Peter Teoh, Shawn Thorpe, Joe Timmins, Tyme, Uluç Ülgen, Unparalleled Suffering Photography, Kimber VanRy, Holly Vear, Laura Vlahovich, Wendy Werneth, John Whiteside, Greg Wise, Darnell Witt, Marc S. Wood, Frank York, and Jason Young.

If you'd like to be a part of future work like *The Animal Show*, please consider joining my Patreon community at patreon.com/michaelharren.

The Animal Show, *The Animal Book*, and *The Animal Album* were all funded in part through the tremendous generosity of A Well Fed World, a hunger relief and animal protection organization chipping away at two of the world's most immense, unnecessary and unconscionable forms of suffering... the suffering of people hungry from lack of food, and the suffering of animals used and abused for food. Find out more about their work at awfw.org.

ABOUT THE ARTIST

Brooklyn-based composer and performer Michael Harren combines elements of classical composition with experimental electronics and storytelling to create hypnotic and boldly intimate work that walks the line between Laurie Anderson, Peter Gabriel and Dead Can Dance. He is artist-in-residence at Tamerlaine Farm Animal Sanctuary where he created the solo multi-media theater piece *The Animal Show*, which premiered in New York City in 2016 and continues to be performed in venues throughout the United States.

In his first solo show, *Tentative Armor*, he combined piano, synthesizers, various electronics, and live musicians with his unique storytelling, resulting in a deeply moving, highly entertaining performance. Through his resonant, powerful, very personal stories, Harren envelops the audience in a funny, poignant, highly intimate tour of his own self-discovery through spirituality, sexuality, and grief. Music, text and photos from the show were released in an album and book of the same name.

Michael Harren has toured as pianist with Sandra Bernhard, is the musical director for Cabaret for a Cause, and has performed at Dixon Place, (le) poisson rouge, Joe's Pub, Judson Memorial Church, Manhattan Theater Source, The Duplex, Don't Tell Mama, The Laurie Beechman Theater as well as numerous venues around the country. Michael is a Moogfest artist who presented *No Permission Needed: Create* with Senator Jaiz at Moogfest 2017.

also by Michael Harren

The Animal Album
Glorious
Tentative Armor, book and album

also published by bd-studios.com

the immeasurable fold: selected poems 2000–2015 by luke kurtis
Georgia Dusk by Dudgrick Bevins & luke kurtis
Angkor Wat book and album by luke kurtis
Visions of the Beyond by Stefanie Masciandaro
Puertas Españolas by Josemaria Mejorada & May Gañán
Jordan's Journey by Jordan M. Scoggins
Just One More by Jonathan David Smyth
Retrospective by Michael Tice

www.ingramcontent.com/pod-product-compliance
Lightning Source LLC
Chambersburg PA
CBHW042350030426
42336CB00025B/3430